Yucky Vegetables

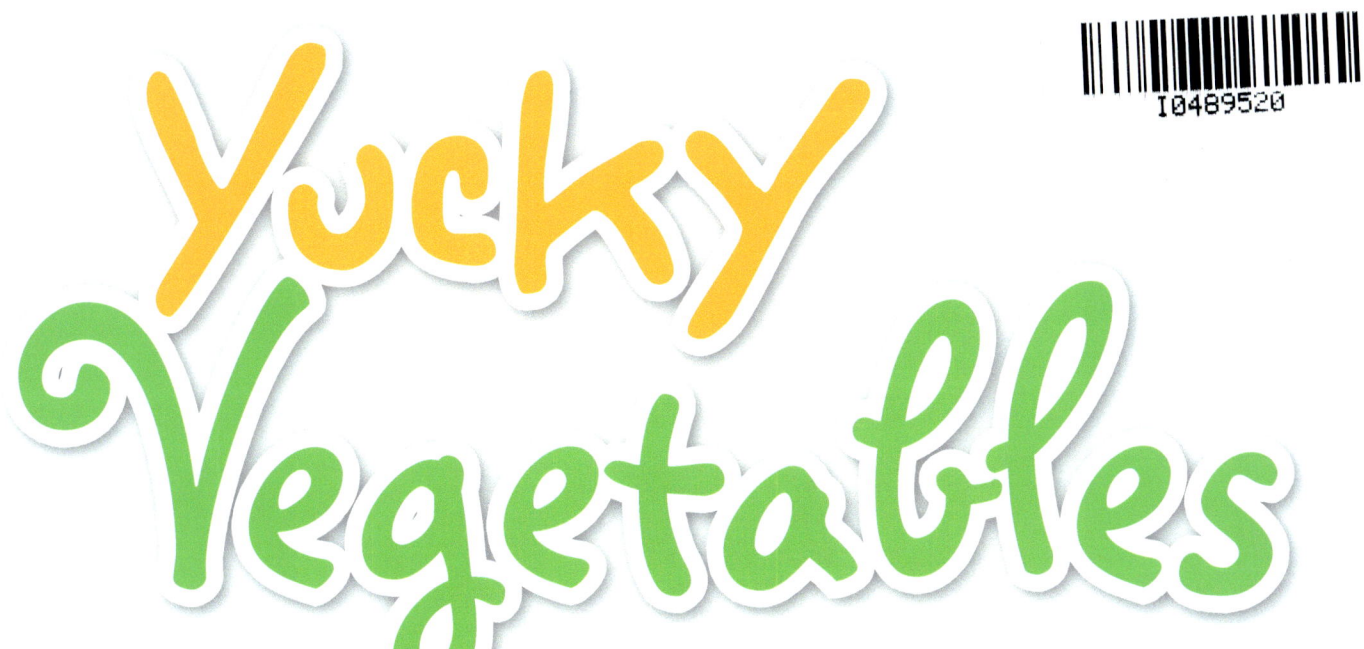

How to Bring Fun and Laughter into Eating Veggies

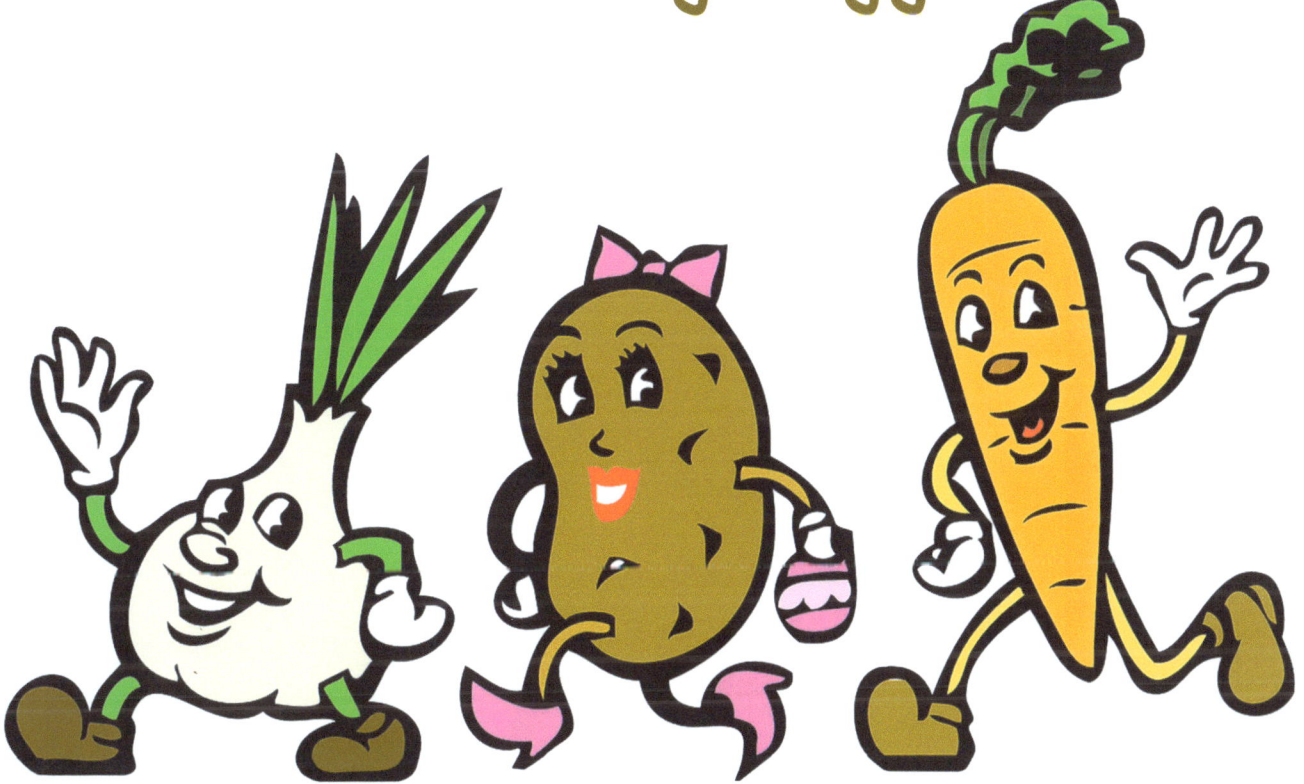

Lavondia Aleem

Yucky Vegetables

How to Bring Fun and Laughter
into Eating Veggies

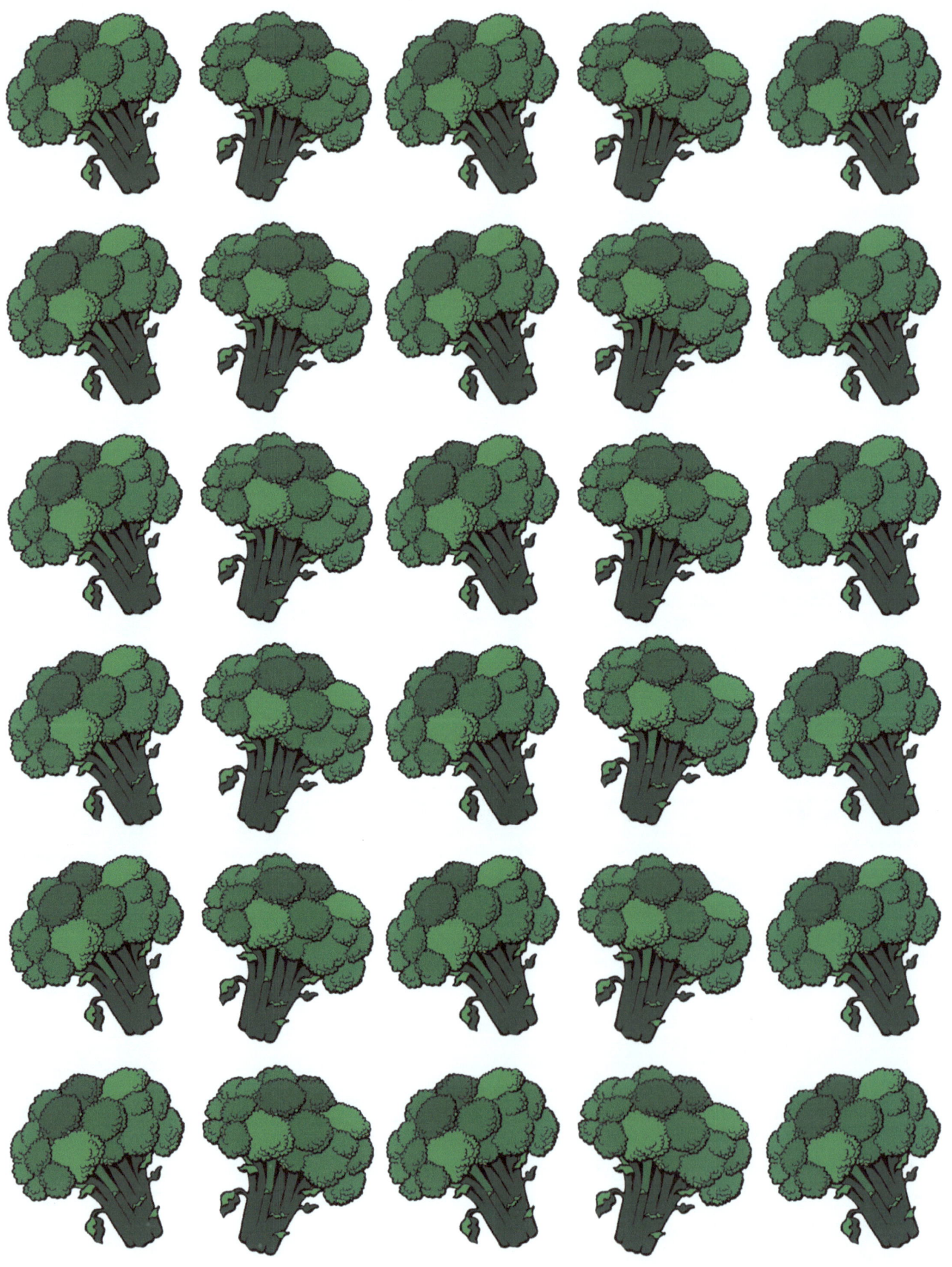

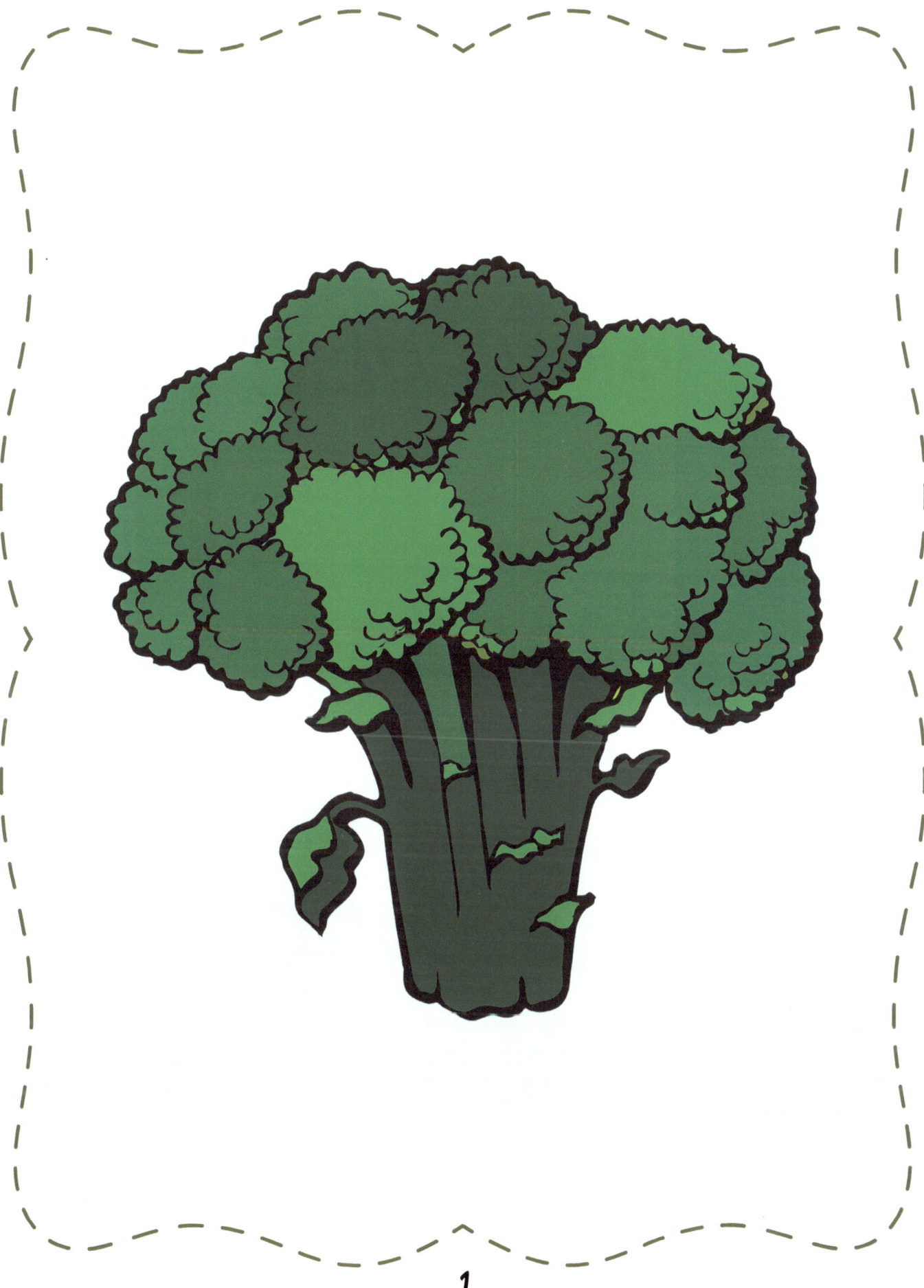

BROCCOLI!

BROCCOLI!

BROCCOLI!

Hey... did you know that broccoli was my favorite food
Until it made me jump out of my shoes.
They are little balls of greeny veggies
 that nourish my body and help me grow...
Sometimes, it looks like my big toe.

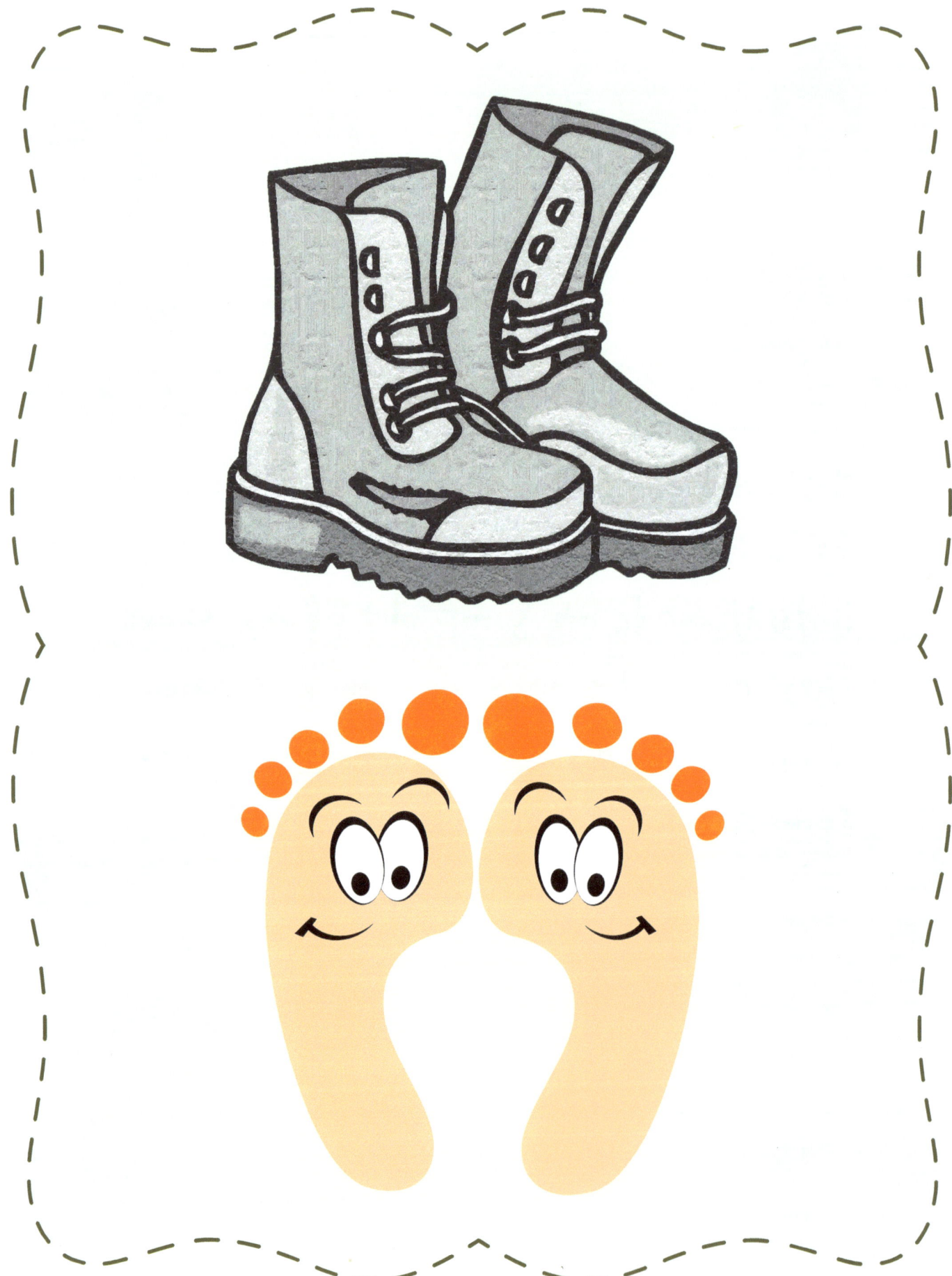

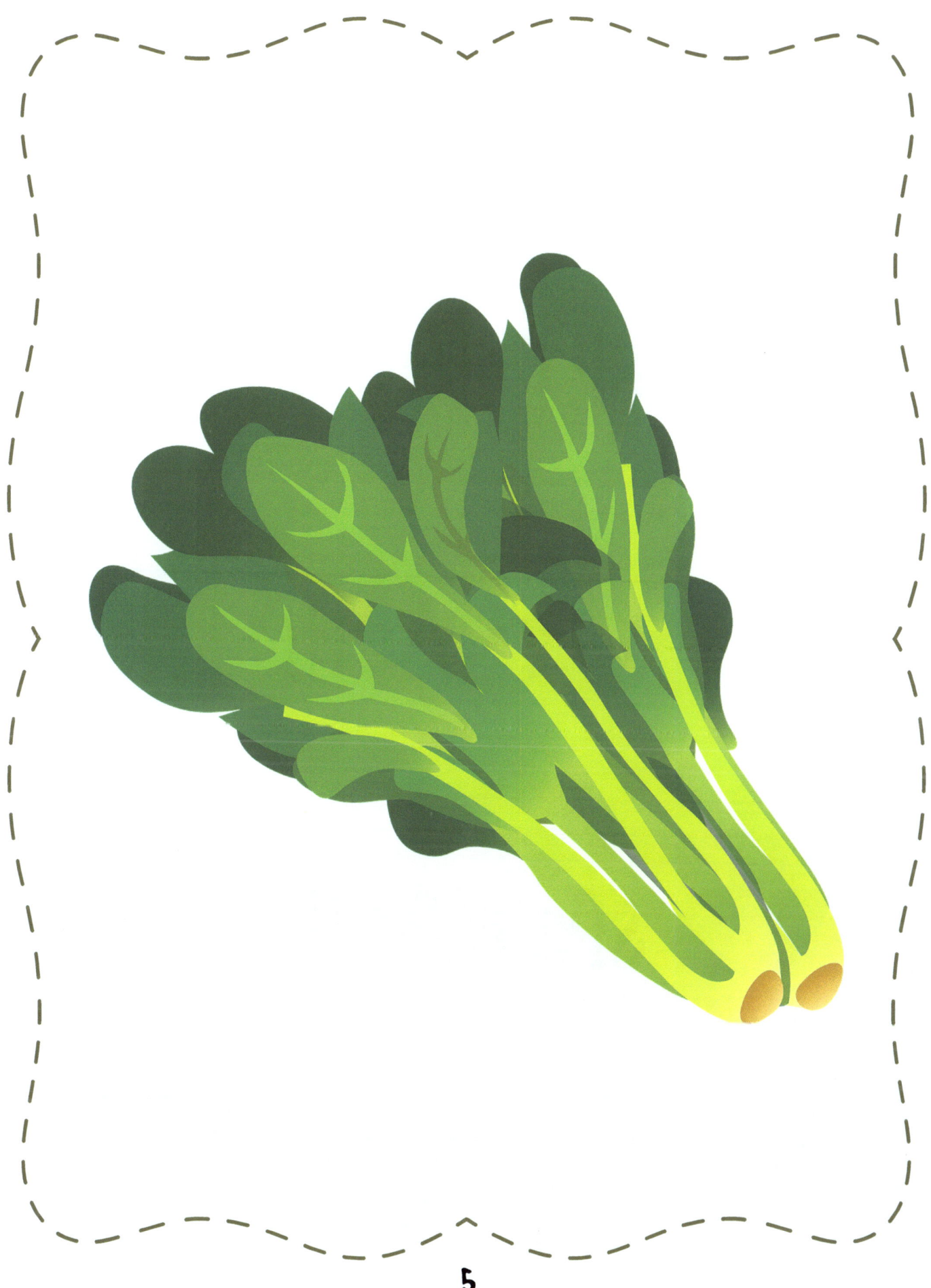

SPINACH!

SPINACH!

SPINACH!

Now I like my spinach better.

Since I discovered it's use as a feather.

I use my fork to twirl it around...

My mom never saw it hit the ground.

It's tastes like a wiggle worm but when

I eat it I feel like a bird.

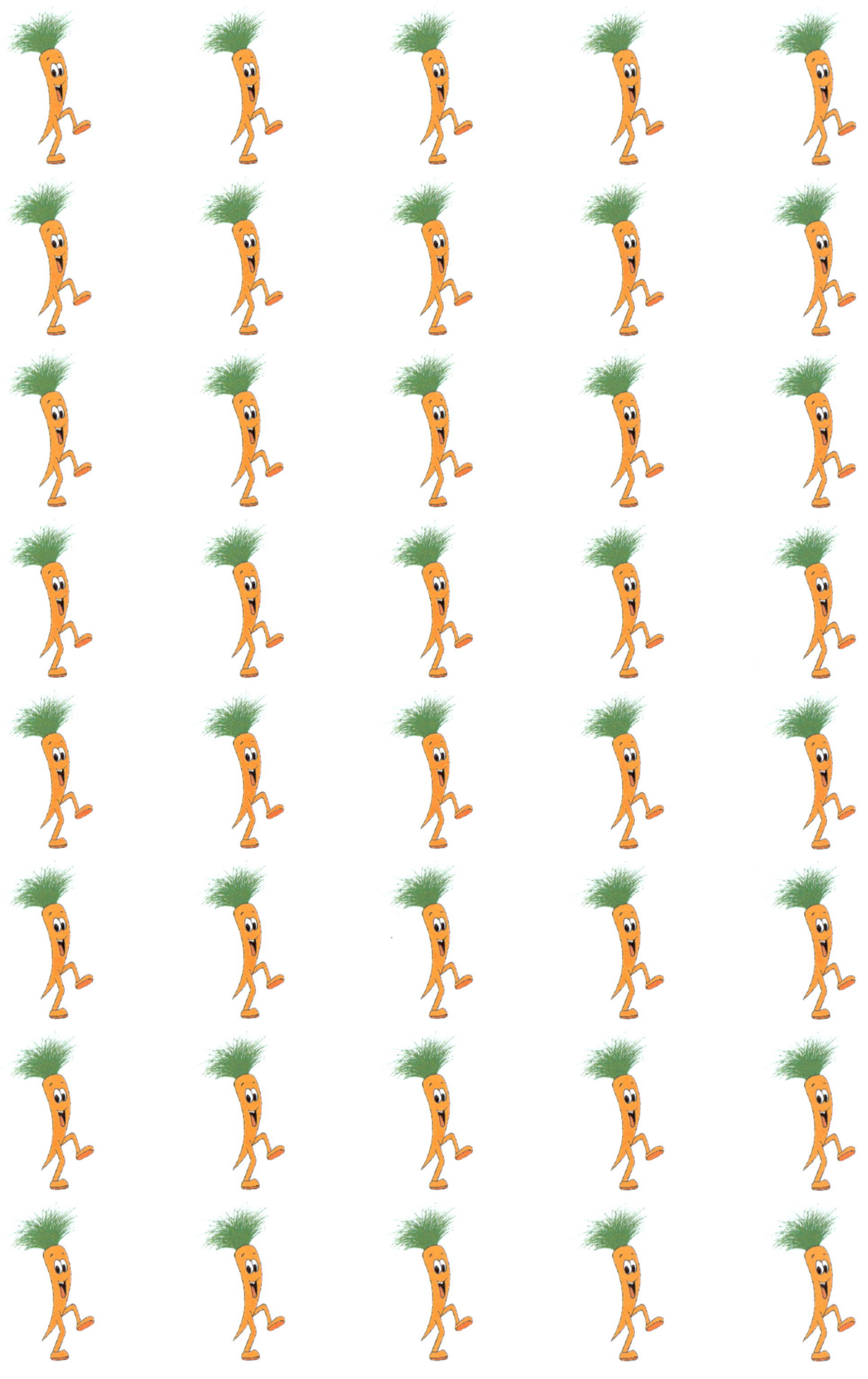

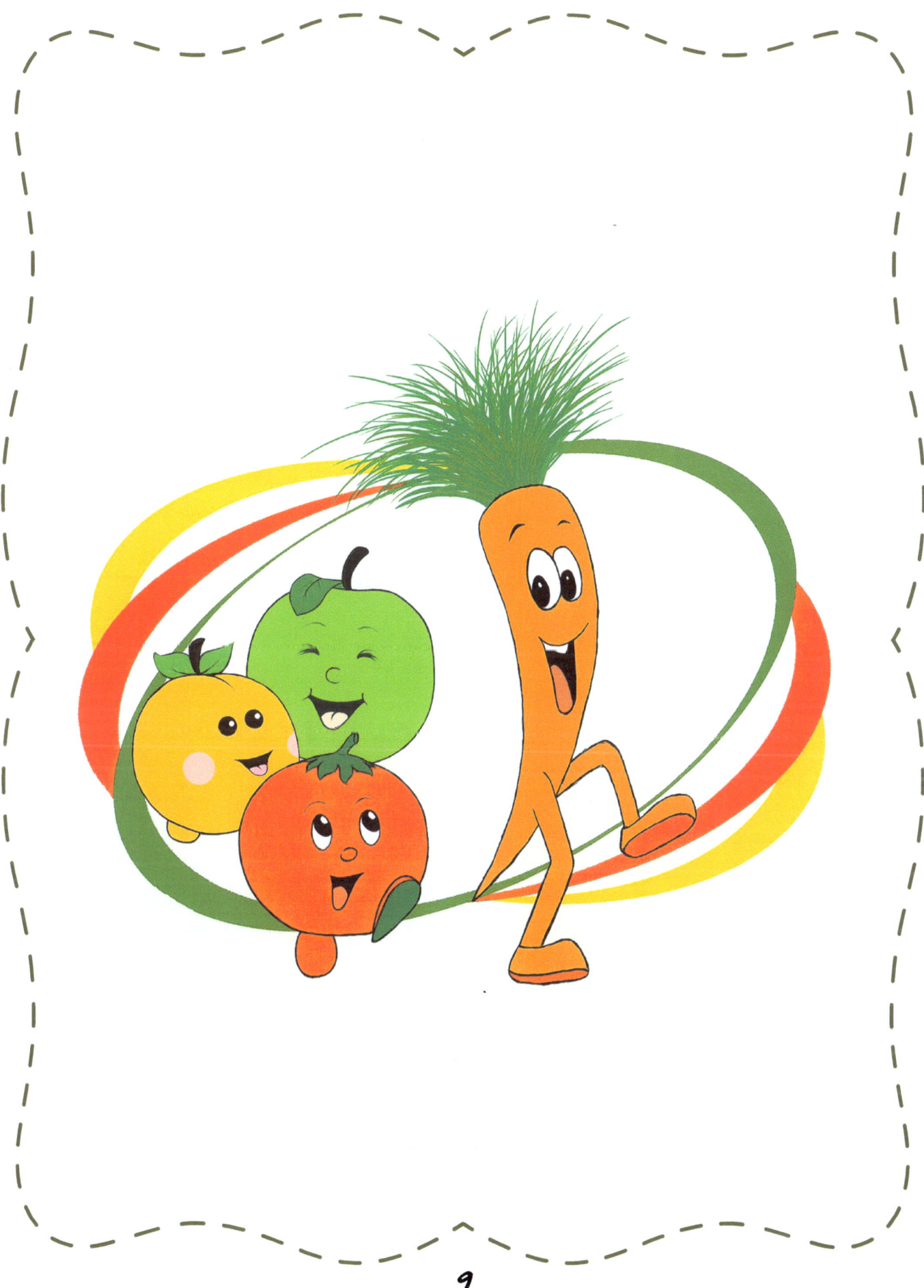

CARROT!

CARROT!

CARROT!

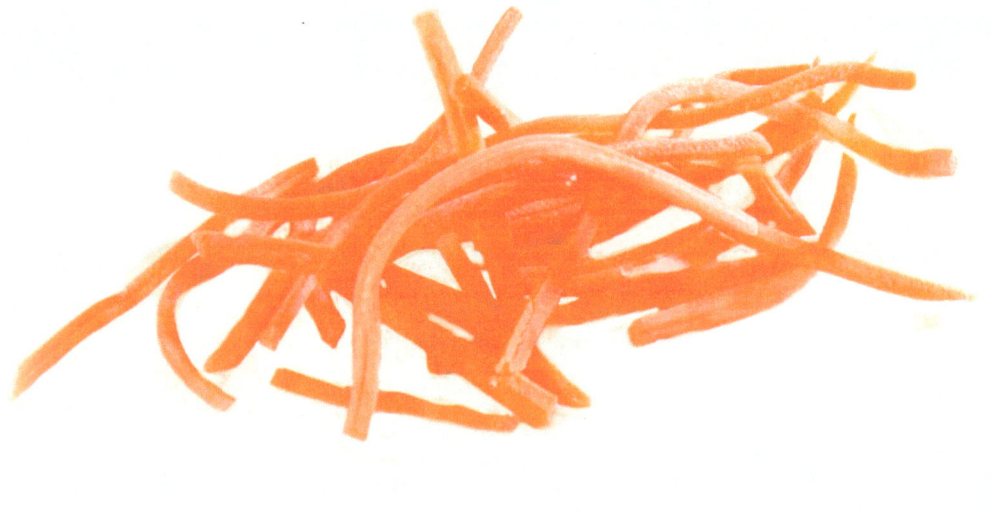

My mom thinks carrots are good for
my eyes
When she turns her head...she's going to
be surprised.
At last, I ate all my veggies even when
I thought I wasn't ready.

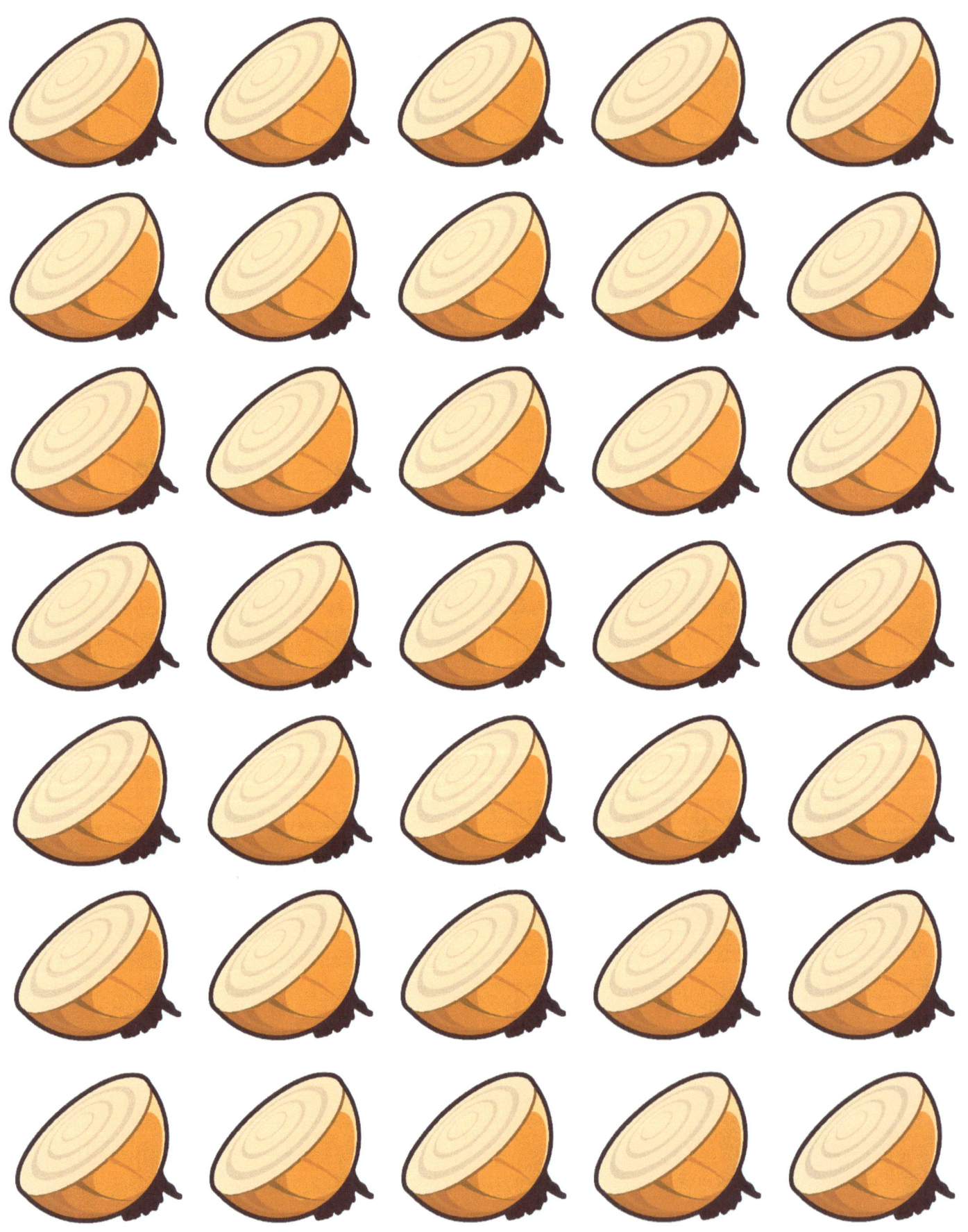

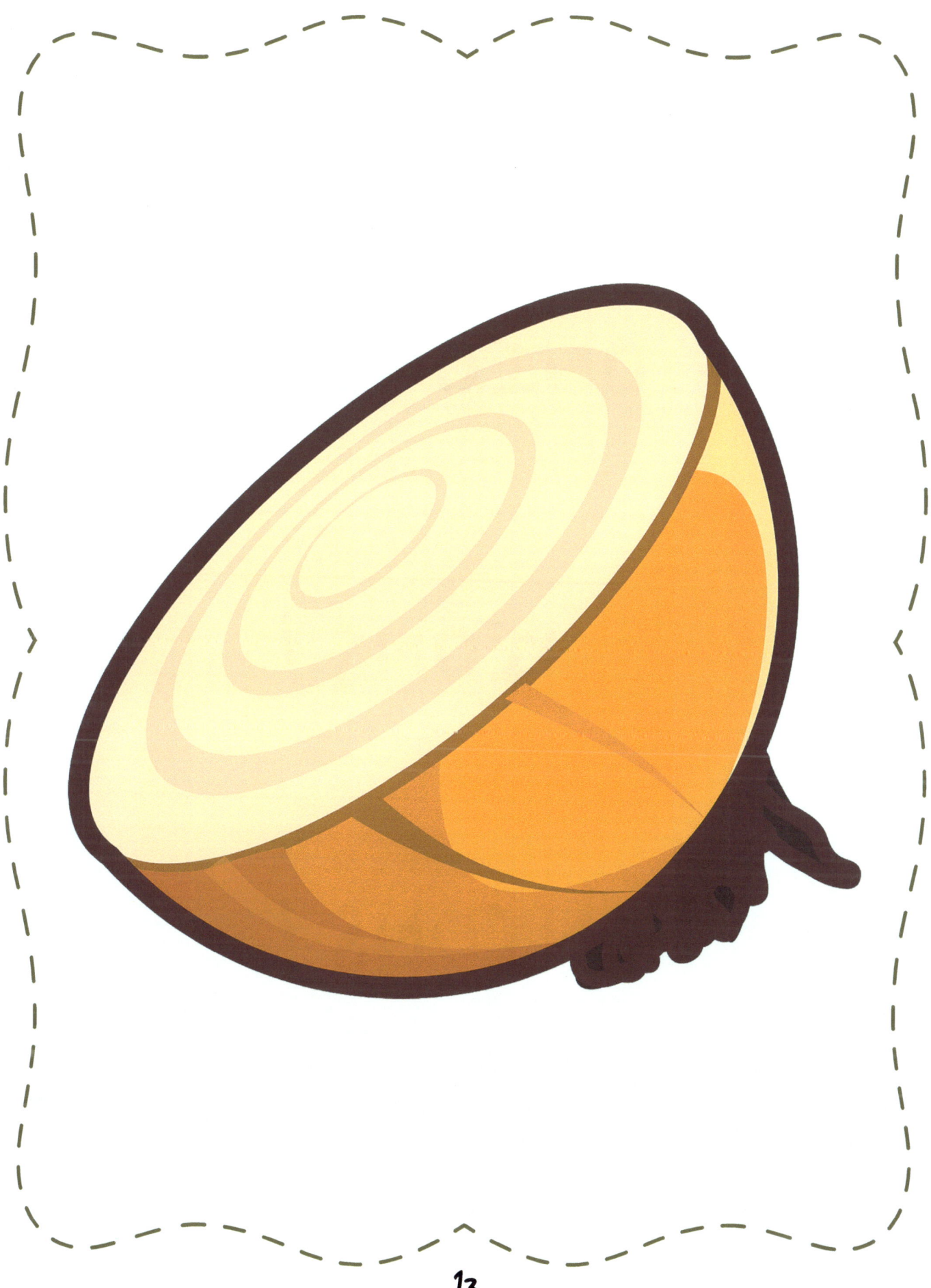

13

ONIONS !

ONIONS !

ONIONS !

Then there are those yellow, smelly onions
I think they look so very funny.
Leaf here and leaf there
I think I will toss them everywhere.
Now I will Growwwwwwww!!!!!!!!

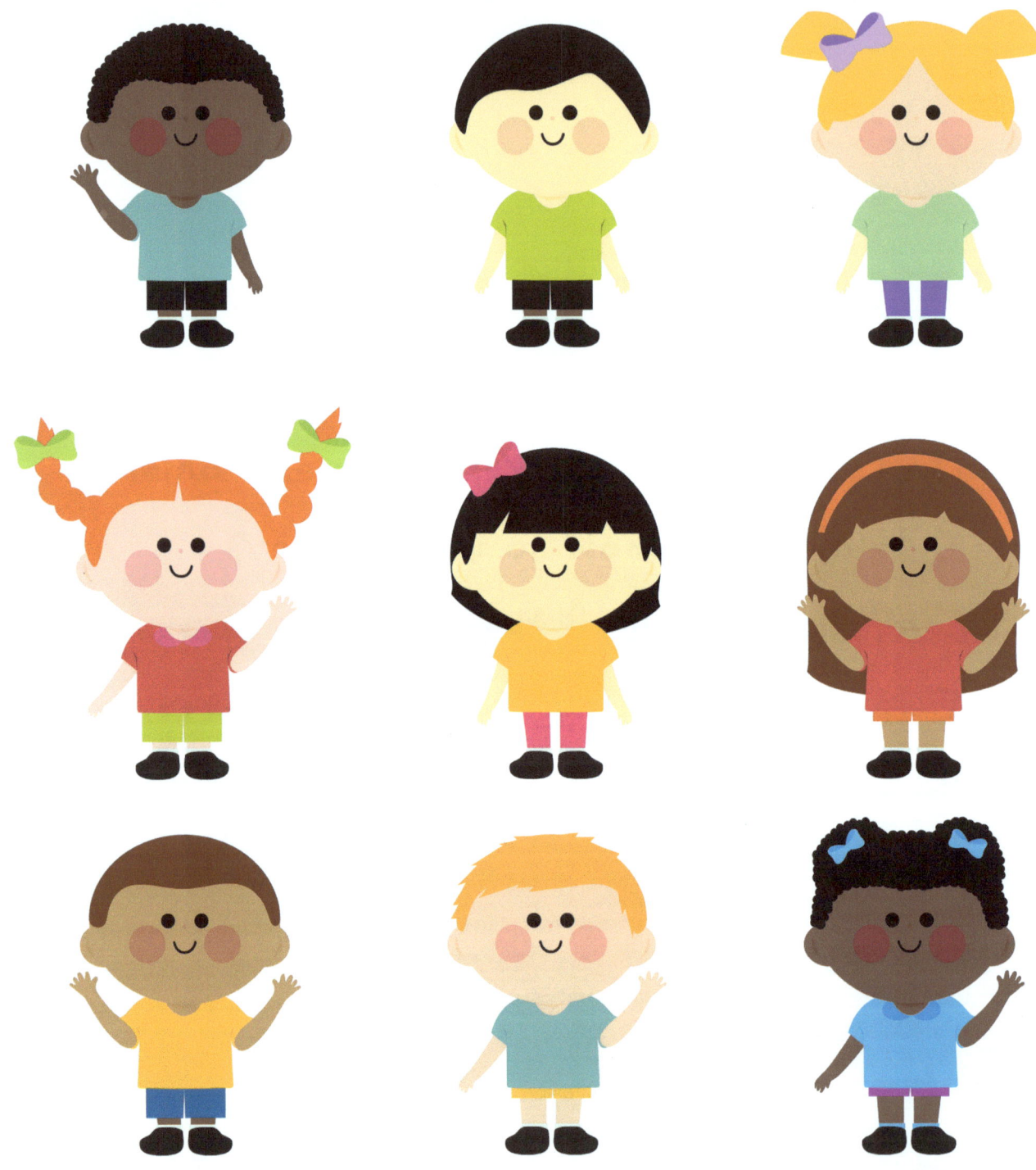

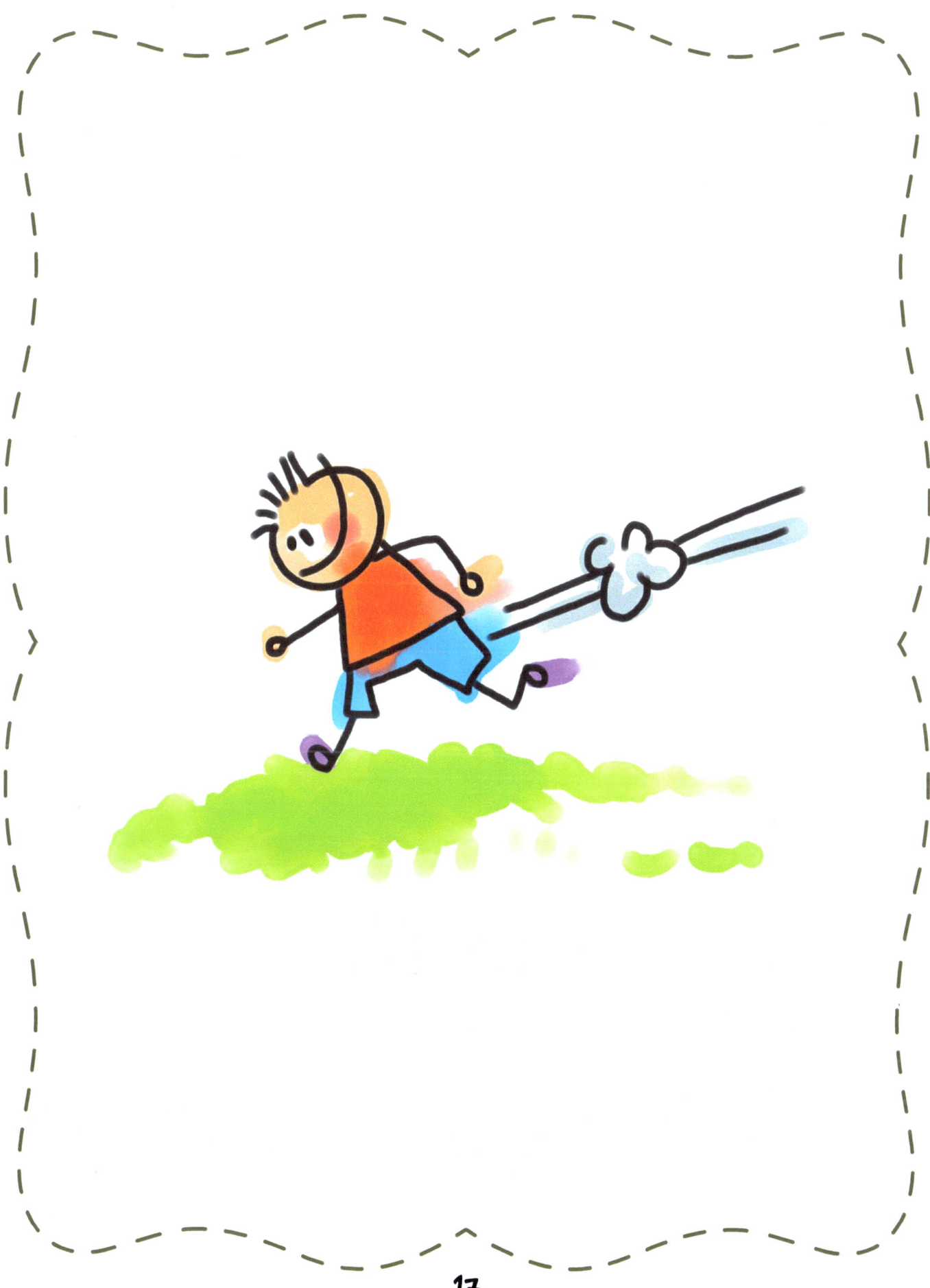

GROW !

GROW !

GROW!

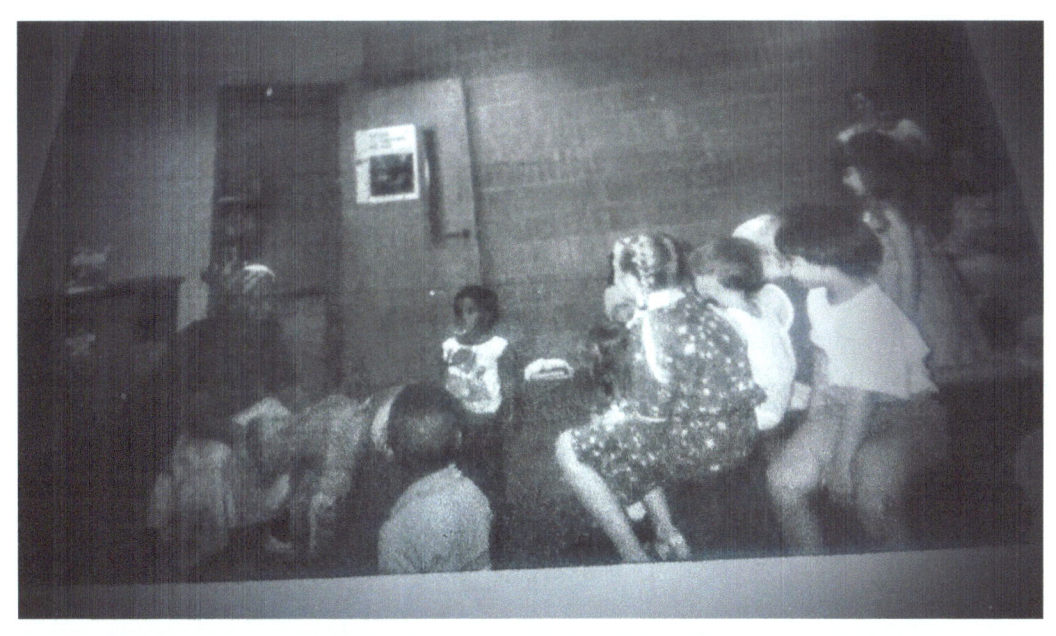

This story is for all ages, those who enjoy having fun with their vegetables. The vegetable story makes them laugh and think about eating more nourishing food. Yucky is how they feel about vegetables anyway, but laughter adds fun to eating their vegetables.

www.ingramcontent.com/pod-product-compliance
Lightning Source LLC
Chambersburg PA
CBHW050439180526
45159CB00006B/2598